HOUSE
Through the Ages

PHILIP STEELE

Illustrated by
ANDREW HOWAT and GORDON DAVIDSON

D1401695

Troll Associates

Library of Congress Cataloging-in-Publication Data

Steele, Philip
    House through the ages / by Philip Steele, illustrated by Andrew
Howat and Gordon Davidson
        p.   cm
    Summary: Describes a succession of human habitations in western
Europe as they represent the development of civilization over
thousands of years, from the caves of Stone Age hunters to modern
apartment houses.
    ISBN 0-8167-2733-3 (lib. bdg.)   ISBN 0-8167-2734-1 (pbk.)
    1. Dwellings–History–Juvenile literature.   [1. Dwellings–
History.   2. Civilization–History.]   I. Howat, Andrew, ill.
II. Davidson, Gordon, ill.   III. Title.
GT172.S74   1993
392.36–dc20   91-36481

Published by Troll Associates
© 1994 Eagle Books

Design by James Marks

Printed in the U.S.A.

10 9 8 7 6 5 4 3 2 1

Introduction

The Earth is forever changing. New
rocks are forced upward from the
depths of the planet, only to be worn
away by wind, rain, and ice. Over the
ages, vast seas have flooded the land,
leaving behind an ooze of mud and
shells. These harden into rock over
millions of years. Plants grow in the soil
as it is warmed by the sun.

Rocks, soil, and plants are valuable
resources. For thousands of years clay,
slate, and stone, as well as timber,
reeds, and straw, have been used as
building materials. They have provided
shelter and warmth for humans.

Our story takes place somewhere in
Western Europe. As you'll see, the story
of housing is the story of human inven-
tiveness and skill.

Contents

Cave dwellers

It had been a long and bitter winter. The hunting band had already buried five of their number in shallow graves in the icy ground. After three weeks of wandering, the hunters came to a high limestone ridge rising above the forest. Open caves gaped like black holes in the hillside.

The caves did not look very inviting, but the hunters were cold and exhausted. They needed shelter. They crawled deep into the darkness, sniffing for the scent of cave bear. Sure enough, there was a terrible growling and snarling in the depths of the cave. But the hunters were prepared, and they killed the powerful animal.

Later, fire brought warmth to the cave, and skins shielded the entrance from the blizzards. The hunters took the skull of the bear and stuck it above the cave as their badge, or totem. The animal's bravery would bring them luck in the future.

Remains of people like these who lived in 50,000 B.C. were first found in the Neanderthal valley of Germany. They were short and powerfully built, with heavy brows and broad faces.

Tents and caves

Summer was spent hunting deer. Large herds passed this way each year. Hunters set up camp at the entrance to a narrow ravine and lay in ambush as the herd approached.

These hunters, who lived in 12,000 B.C., were of slighter build than the Neanderthal people, who had left the region thousands of years before. They were more cunning, too. Summer shelters were probably built of birch poles covered in leaves or animal skins. The skins were tied to the poles with thongs, and the borders were weighted down with boulders. Tents of this kind were later perfected in the Indian *tepee* of the North American plains. Many peoples today are still tent dwellers.

Some of the caves were used for magic rituals. Before the hunters left in the spring, they dressed in animal skins and horns and danced for good luck.
The walls of the cave were decorated with pictures of bisons, stags, and boars. The paint was made of red and yellow ocher, and of soot or charcoal mixed with fat.

During the winter snows, the tribe returned to the caves on the ridge. The roofs of some caves were now blackened by the soot of many fires, and the earth of the floor was trampled flat. Lamps of animal fat gave out a flickering glow. The caves were gloomy, but they offered protection from attack.

Homes on the lake

By about 10,000 B.C., the weather had become warmer. The marshy lowlands to the south of the ridge became a maze of lakes and waterways. For thousands of years, these waters were fished by hunters with spears and bone fishhooks.

By 1100 B.C., hunters had learned to mix copper with tin to make bronze. They used bronze to make tools, such

as axes. Some hunters built a village on an island in one of the lakes. The lake provided both food and safety from attack by the fierce mountain tribes.

Building materials were ferried out from the mainland in a boat hollowed from a tree trunk. The dwellings were protected by a wall of sharp stakes driven into the mud of the lake.

The chief's house was a fine log cabin, with three rooms and a porch. The roof was thatched with reeds. Inner walls were made of wattle and daub (interwoven hazel sticks plastered with mud and straw). Smaller houses had only one or two rooms. There were also outhouses, grain-storage buildings, workshops, and sheep pens.

9

Celtic huts

The lake village had been swept away in the spring floods of 850 B.C. Many people and animals had drowned. New warriors ruled the land by 300 B.C. These were the Celts, who had mastered the secrets of iron.

The chieftain had his headquarters high on the ridge, defended by great earthworks. Many huts were built near this hill fort. When war threatened, the warriors took their families and prized possessions up to

the safety of the hill fort before fighting began.

Each house was about 50 feet (15 meters) from side to side. The roof was large and cone-shaped, made of timbers covered with branches and sod. A thick thatch of straw was attached to this. The roof was supported by tall, thick pillars. The round outer walls were often made of timber. Inside, small rooms of wattle and daub surrounded a central hall and hearth. The floor was covered with rushes. People ate at low wooden tables and slept on soft animal skins.

It was dark inside the huts. Smoke escaped through a hole in the roof, but it blew back and stung the eyes on windy days. Wheat, barley, and oats were stored in separate huts. These were raised off the ground to protect the grain from rats and rising damp.

A Roman villa

When the Romans invaded the region in A.D. 80, the Celts could scarcely believe their eyes. Their conquerors were brilliant architects and engineers. They used bricks, tiles, mortar, and stone for building. By 350, most of the Celts had grown used to the ways of Rome. However, none of them could afford to live in houses like this villa. It was built for a rich Roman, who had been banished to this remote place.

Construction on this villa began in 300. It had an entrance hall and a dining room decorated with murals, or wall paintings. It had living rooms, bedrooms, saunas, baths, and toilets.

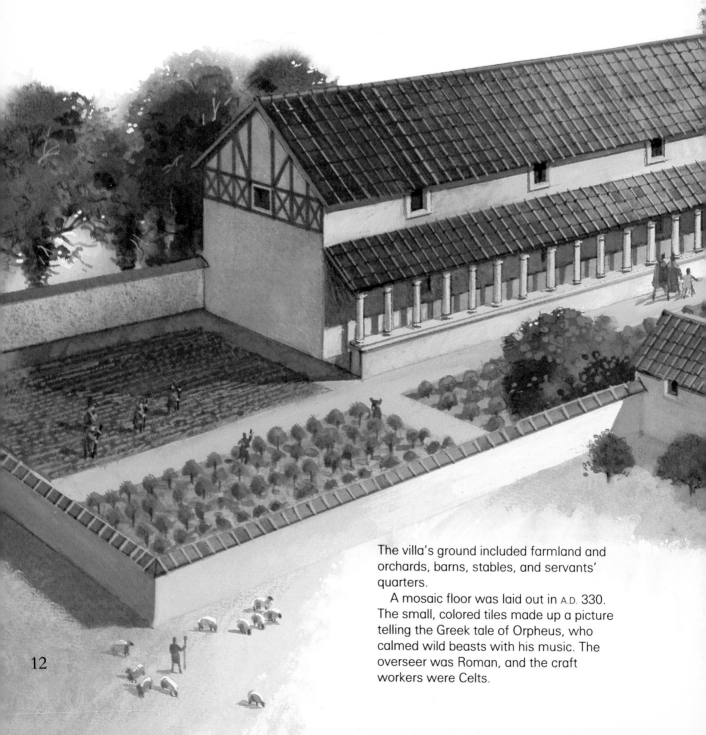

The villa's ground included farmland and orchards, barns, stables, and servants' quarters.

A mosaic floor was laid out in A.D. 330. The small, colored tiles made up a picture telling the Greek tale of Orpheus, who calmed wild beasts with his music. The overseer was Roman, and the craft workers were Celts.

Ducts from a boiler carried heat beneath the villa's floors and out through flues in the walls. This was the first known form of central heating, unmatched for over 1,600 years.

13

A Viking longhouse

Toward the end of the fourth century, barbaric tribes attacked the region. The villa was burned down, and Romans and Celts alike sought shelter in the old hill fort. The Roman soldiers were soon ordered back to Rome, which was also under attack from other warrior bands.

Years of battle and hardship followed. In the ninth century, warriors from Scandinavia raided the region. Summer after summer, the long ships of these Viking pirates rowed up the river. In 900, a small group stayed behind and built a new settlement, defended by earthworks and a timber fence.

The Viking longhouses were large halls built of timber or stone and wattle and daub. Windows had wooden shutters. The walls were hung with tapestries, and the floor covered with rushes. Light came from oil lamps or flickering torches. The longhouse included food-storage areas and rooms for spinning and weaving, but no real bedrooms. Most people slept on benches in the main hall.

At a great feast, the warriors hung their shields and swords on the wall and sat on benches at long tables. A harpist played and sang, and told riddles and tales.

Stone and timber

The Viking settlement burned down in 950 when a spark from the blacksmith's shop set a roof on fire. In 1050, the region was invaded again. The newcomers were also of Viking origin, but their ancestors had settled in the Normandy region of France.

The Normans built a wooden fortress on a large mound above the old Viking settlement. This was later converted into a huge castle with thick walls of locally quarried stone. The castle was built for defense rather than comfort. The high-ceilinged stone halls were drafty and cold even when logs were blazing in the large fireplaces.

A small town grew up, surrounded by the castle's outer walls. It had a fine stone church, but most of the houses still were made of timber. Many houses still had thatched roofs. But new roofs were supposed to be made of tile to reduce the risk of fire.

In 1250, the street was full of hauling tackle, pulleys, and wooden scaffolding. One of the richest merchants in the town was having a new house built. It was to be constructed of stone, and so he hired the best masons in the region. Some of them had worked on the town's new church.

The growing town

By 1600 the town was growing larger, but most of the houses were still made of timber. The spaces between the oak timbers were filled with wattle and daub or with bricks. Bricks were now often used for walls and paving.

A building's upper floors, or stories, often hung over the street to protect the lower walls from rain. A few houses had windows made of small panes of glass set in lead.

Water had to be fetched and carried and the large houses in town needed many servants. Wood was still commonly used for heating and cooking, but was in short supply. Much of the ancient forest had been cut down. There was no coal in the area, but some was carried down the coast by ship. This "sea coal" was burned in many houses. High chimneys were built to carry fumes away from the houses.

Because houses were built of wood and streets were narrow, the risk of fire was great. Many houses burned to the ground during a fire in 1650. The town was rebuilt in stone, with wider streets.

Walking in the street was hazardous. There was no proper drainage or sewage system. Water and garbage were simply tossed out of windows or dumped into the gutter.

The Nabob's house

Nobody knew where the gentleman came from, or how he made his money. They only knew he had spent some time trading in India, where he became rich enough to retire while he

The house was built in 1700 on solid stone foundations. Wooden cross beams, or joists, supported floors and ceilings.

was still young. Like others of his background, he was nicknamed "the Nabob," after a Hindi word for governor.

The Nabob bought a fine house on the edge of the town, but he had a large country estate as well. The gossipers collecting water at the town pump disliked his haughty manner, but agreed that he ran a fine house.

In the Nabob's home, tea was sipped from the finest china, and there were curtains of rich brocade at the windows. One room was a small library, with books bound in leather. In the hallway, a tall grandfather clock chimed the hours. After dark, candlelight gleamed off wooden paneling, polished tables, and silver. The four-poster bed was warmed by a long-handled pan of copper filled with glowing coals and placed between the sheets. Servants' quarters were in the attic and the basement.

Terraced housing

By 1870 the old town had become a great city. Factory chimneys poured out clouds of smoke that darkened the sky. Laundry left to dry on the clothes-line sometimes became covered in black soot.

The factory owner had a grand house, surrounded by a leafy park. The manager lived comfortably too.

The company built large numbers of terraced houses that were rented out to the factory workers. The red-brick buildings were small and poorly built, with small back yards. There were no indoor bathrooms. Water was heated on a long iron stove in the small kitchen.

Roofs were covered in gray slate, which was quarried locally. Rainwater collected in iron gutters and flowed away down pipes into the main drains. Drains and sewers had been built under the city.

Life in the shadow of the factory was hard. People were poor and their diet was bad. However, everybody knew each other and offered a helping hand when times were difficult.

Suburban homes

During the 1930s, the city spread farther and farther into the countryside, forming suburbs. There were new roads and railroads. People could travel into the center of the city to work each day. Many of the suburbs were built near parks and tree-lined roads, far from the factory chimneys and smoke.

Many houses had small gardens and garages for cars. Sometimes two houses were joined together. Some had wide metal windows, which were mass-produced in factories and then installed at the building site. New building materials included concrete reinforced with steel.

Homes had running water, indoor bathrooms, and carpeted floors. Electricity was used for lighting and to power all kinds of appliances. Vacuum cleaners cleaned floors quickly. Some homes had refrigerators to keep food cold, and some even had central heating. Many still burned logs and coal in open grates.

Radios kept people in touch with the outside world.

Skyscrapers

Skyscrapers had been built in the United States since the 1880s, but it was 1955 before high office buildings began to appear in this city. The first high-rise apartment building was built in the suburbs in 1959.

Huge cranes towered above the building site. A noisy pile driver hammered long tubes of steel deep into the earth. These piles supported a tall framework of columns and steel beams, or girders. The outside shell of the building was made of reinforced concrete sections. These were prefabricated, which means they had already been made before building work started. Large windows were made of strong plate glass. Each apartment was centrally heated and comfortably furnished. There were two bedrooms, a living room, a small kitchen, and a bathroom.

The apartment was on the ninth floor, and sometimes the elevator was broken. There was nowhere for the children to play, and few places to meet the neighbors for a chat. Many people felt lonely in these apartments.

27

The present

During the 1980s, many of the high-rise blocks were demolished. There were still skyscrapers in the city center – gleaming offices of steel and mirrored glass.

The factories had been demolished long ago. By the old ship canal, warehouses were being renovated.

New luxurious houses were built. Many local people could no longer afford to buy or rent property in this district, and had to move away.

A businesswoman moved into one new apartment. She worked from